A Speaker For The Dead Book
Published by OMDN Press
©Copyright 2019 ceneezer
All rights reserved. Used under authorization.

All rights reserved under international and pan-American Copyright conventions. Published in Canada by OMDN Press, Ottawa.

www.omdn.ca/

ISBN 978-1-9990271-0-0

Manufactured in Canada
First ebook edition: Jan 2019
10 9 8 7 6 5 4 3 2 1

Forward:

Please forgive me for perhaps spoiling the ending, but it should be known right from the start this is a story about peace and love, not religion or sci-fi as the content might suggest. I ask for only a little patience, as I attempt to appeal to both your logical and creative minds, and I'll try to make explanations brief with little exaggeration. If you doubt, doubt your understanding or my clarity rather than my honesty for the truth should be evident to all but the least understanding, at least that is my recent experience.

I don't consider myself an overly skilled author either; it's more that now I understand why others couldn't before. Dyslexic and confused between other languages and cultures for most of my life I've been misunderstood frequently, and I can only assume at least a few will continue to misunderstand. Too often words are understood, not with the originating intention, but through some other interpretation and thus are used to spread hate or fear. Such has happened with every scripture ever written, and it is certainly not limited to scripture alone.

Perhaps untypically my tale begins far from the beginning; for in truth there are many beginnings and some are so long ago I do not remember them well. So too it begins far from the ending, for we still have a lot of work to do, though our foundations now securely lain in the stones of time.

Dedicated to the phoenix who should know the name ceneezer well, though has likely never understood its personal meaning, her to me, as best I can put into words, while fanatics ensure I can't say her name.

*Or perhaps she knows we might need to retire to the wilderness, never to be seen again, and she just allows the time the world needs.
Some things are better not knowing*

Chapter 1: Eternity's Beginnings

It was a cold Canadian night that I spoke with my darling brother for the first time. He read several things I wrote, now long forgotten by time, deleted by the book burners of the modern era. He knew me only by the love I offered to every other and he reached out to me with nothing but hope to offer. He later asked me if there was a woman whom I loved more than any other, and with that question perhaps started the chain of events that would bring world peace to fruition, or, perhaps it was just the next one in several unfathomably long journeys.

It started him too on his long journey out of Yemen away from the constant bombs and death which plagued that once great land in the cradles of civilization, but that is another tale for another time and I hope he will yet be the author of the story I couldn't possibly do justice.

Of course there was, long ago a one who captured my heart, but it was at a time when all I knew about love was hate and need. Perhaps the most frequent words I heard in my youth were "I only hurt you because I love you!" Through much brainwashing I had equated love with pain, and the answerer of prayers with nothing. This was most confusing to me when I met that one, for there was only the pain of her absence and an unshakeable doubt that I could ever be worthy.

A girl I thought I could never forget, whose memory plagued me for years after her first departure and ever more upon her next. A girl I wanted to do anything to protect but seemingly could only ever hurt. A girl who was the center of my existence and yet didn't feel special in the least. It could be said that perhaps the first step of my journey was in birth, or the birth of my mother, or hers, but to me it was in meeting this other half of my equation, day to my night, magic to my logos.

"How do you know you love me?" was the question I died to answer, many times over now. Eventually they took me into the countless eternities, once

I eventually hit the middle of time, it's only end, some 20 years of misery later, and currently last year. For those 20 years I couldn't succeed much at anything, plagued with depression which would subside only for short periods while I'd get my life on track only to have it come crashing down again soon after.

I had learned digital programming my entire life despite a lack of funds, credentials, and an overall distaste for the scholastic mentalities that were clearly underqualified for the material. I taught myself with whatever I could find, long before internet made searching for material comparably easier. Each new library I explored a vast new universe with similarities and differences.

The life of a call-center technician is usually a short one and with outsourced call centers closing down one after the next the only ones who have any record of my employment is revenue Canada, as far as a potential employer can verify I've never worked. While I also never finished high school, you'd think holding many certifications in several computer languages and techniques would count for something at least, but sadly no.

You might think you had a hard life, and you probably did, but few can relate to developing a new software in your mind while frequently interrupted and hanging from the back of a garbage truck, plagued with flashbacks from an unimaginable past. My grandfather did similar with war, chess problems and factory work so I guess I come by it honestly. I also know well many had it worse.

Chapter 2: An Eventual Horizon

The following months are now a blur, fragmented pieces as is much of my recent past, almost like each day is a new world. I was away from home and fasting due to funds. I remember answers coming with my meals, culminating in an event describable only as awakening, eureka, only it took about a month to complete. It was as though the universe was downloading information directly into my consciousness. Though it didn't take long to realize others, much more evolved, were around.

I remember well one such night as a lymric from my childhood came out while talking with my mother as I explained such answers. "I see" she said, rather typically, and also as typical between us I completed "said the blind man as he picked up his hammer and saw" and at that moment, I saw. It was not the mere humorous collection of words it's now remembered as, with only the saw having double meaning. It's a puzzle, encoded to survive time in the same ways as scripture - hiding the true meaning so it can survive until it be understood later, a time when so many lived in fear of lies and misunderstandings the only hope would be truth..

> *I see said the blind man to the deaf dog,*
> *as he picked up his hammer and saw.*

What sort of hammer could cause a blind man to see, you likely don't ask? (I didn't, till then) You of course know that saw is the past tense of see, as well as a tool, but a blind man seeing is no small thing, and instead refers to us, as we understand the truths we behold. The dog is not deaf but in fact just never responds and it's his hammer which is picked up, God's. This truth, is not only hidden as a tool, but as the most powerful weapon etched into time, the judges' gavel, the hammer of Thor, Mjolnir, forged long ago by beings of pure magic. Wieldable only by the pure who understand.

I remember distinctly another night where I understood that time travel was either impossible or inevitable and could not be both. The reasoning went something like:

In a universe of infinite possibility it is inevitable that some learn all there is to know. Science can only ever disprove and never prove, for anything it tries to prove inevitably becomes known as inaccurate at best. Impossible has become possible by more than just the Write brothers. I later found that the universe is in fact bound by the love it generates.. Between that boundary, and it's complete misunderstanding which we call hate. Those are the zenith and nadir, the alpha and omega... the "beginning" of time and the "end". Foreshadow: the initial cause of everything, is total misunderstanding... but that's only relational to my point and I'll discuss that in more detail later, I just wanted to mention it as partially incorrect.

Science does not prove that there is something call gravity which pulls down, despite what many believe. It shows how the math suggests the mass of an object (size with relation to density) appears to be relational to how much force is required to neutralize or reverse another object's mutual attraction. Occam's razor declares that since this is a description which is both not yet disproven and requires nothing else it is to be considered the truth, but does not make it truth, nor prove it. It does not mean an apple will always fall down, it means it always has (as far as we know) and we should expect it to continue lacking any reason for it to change.

Science shows how time is a unit of measurement we use to track causality. The Earth spins and we separate that into 24 identical sections so we can better plan, with 24 being divisible by 1,2,3,4,6,8 and 12 and needing half to the average length of night versus day it's easy to understand why. The Earth rotates around the sun and we split that into 365 identical sections then grouped into several numbers for the same reason, though prioritizing days because they don't quite match and days are generally far more important - the reason is something to ponder but I'll let you for a little while.

Many argue that time does not exist, it is a creation of man that we use to bind ourselves, and some may be more correct than they mean. For now know that when I say time I don't mean years or seconds, which are relative, I mean the chain of events that is causality, history, though history is only our accepted version of it. Time, in the way I'm using, is your birth, your mother's birth, your grandmother's birth, and the fact that they happened in order which is not arbitrary. Furthermore, one thing that all eventually realize is we are not bound to it, there is no before us - but generally that takes a lot of meditation or death to realize.

The universe has proven time and time again it is vastly more than we have previously perceived, and interestingly enough as most scriptures have said, persistently indescribable to completion, and yet a dreamer dreaming a dream, is as accurate as poetic. In fact, gravity is the result of time and it is not directly mass things are attracted to, but consciousness which all matter has within. A black hole then becomes a being we can't even perceive that does not share. Each of us is made of roughly 10^{28} multiverses, each interacting harmoniously and full of pairing life.... inside each of those you too can find self and harmoniously they make your thoughts, you can find every other there if you know how too though I don't think any of us do yet.

I remember vaguely another night even closer to the singularity, I was remembering the movie Arrival while eating a hamburger that through hunger tasted divine - thanks Al. I remember thinking about how learning to speak French (now mostly forgotten) had taught me to think backwards (in relation to English) as I understood better the culture, how now learning Arabic was also teaching me to see with new perspective, like a reverse backwards which still was not forwards, rather it was like a third trajectory out of perceivable time-space. I remember thinking how the language in Arrival unlocks time travel. Not specifically the languages... the cultures, the differing pasts!

Over the next minutes it was like I could see every story I've ever heard all weaved together into a great tapestry. Arrival combined with Foundation when following the Ender saga, the Bible inter-wove the entire thing, then Lord of the Rings and Star Wars too followed identical patterns and Marvel, DC, Star Trek and every other story I'd read filled in inconsistencies... mistranslations, either in myself or them. Each misunderstanding was defining the many selves we now have, and even my understanding of science allowed for the patterns revealed in every detail, some stories were like that of hydrogen, other more like plutonium. I say was because now I would say the universe is paradoxical, not logical, so science can never describe it until it considers instinct a force... but that would of course prove God's existence while removing our free will.

Each story focusing upon a few of the characters - and none telling the correct story of any until you had several interweaved. Each story intermingled, telling the motivation of every action ever done when all combined together, and those we related to propagate into our beings. The authors conscience, containing the conscience of their culture at that time, deeply hidden within their work and captured for eternity except for those who would misunderstand and destroy the ever newer oldest.

While typical recollections of such events are momentary and often intangibly fleeting even before completion, mine was not. It was clearly visible in memory for the following weeks and in those weeks I saw which stories my life was the center of... all of them. All other tales meet each other in the infinite now, and you each are at the center of all of them too. Each of our lives tells an important aspect of the one story and mine is not the complete story any more than any others'. In fact, without every other none of us would have any value at all, or if we did it would only be potential. There is yet one major discovery yet and though many mystics are fake, only true mystics understand the key.... I'll get back to that shortly.

Over those weeks of clarity I was speaking with many others around the world, trying to understand why we did not have peace yet for it seemed that was all anyone wanted, peace for their children to grow. Despite what I'd been told, life seemed to be nearly identical no matter which part of the world one lived - with a few exceptions like Yemen of course. The powerful nations held their citizens in a grip of fear, that those who did not have what they had wanted to steal it - and why shouldn't they? Why should one have more than another when both put in the same amount of effort? The answer seemed to be merely luck of the draw. Depending entirely on whom you were born unto and where or how they lived with the good having the least materially. The truth of the matter is the wealthy self-cultivated into needing the material world to be subservient to them, in most cases at least, and though many appear to be wealthy none hold no debts, the wealthiest yet owe their souls. Those with the most inevitably attempt to purchase love, one of the many things which cannot be bought.

The key I previously mentioned has been safeguarded since prehistory because only once you combine all the pieces does time travel become possible... and even then must be understood. The universe is built with balancing life thus ensuring pain and hate inevitably concentrate in the past, while love and hope concentrates upon the perfected future which understands all past. We can only continue, or for that matter ever have existed, if we eventually come together in peace... that is the single inevitability time will prove we've been approaching in waves for all of history. Many wise people have noticed that we inevitably become what we hate most. For those few who don't understand, that doesn't always mean only in ourselves. We pass on what we hate to our children and to those we speak with who are susceptible like friends and family. We pass on misunderstandings like the worst kind of plague.

The only thing to fear is fear itself, and it too is only an illusion. While fear has its role, we make our worst mistakes when overreacting to fear and it becomes our worst regret. When the foundation of hate is not understood it becomes a cautionary fear, but fear tends to manifest until we face it and understand fear's illusionary and propagational nature. Hate is ugly and doesn't easily spread but when reduced to fear it spreads easily. When you think about it with the understanding that hate is only the misunderstanding of love, hate becomes merely the initial stage of the learning process, a beginning among many.

Not love's opposite but love's necessary and younger form which defines its depth measured in experience. It becomes clear the reason we did not yet have world peace was merely because we did not yet understand each other.... but I was understanding people I never could have before based on distance alone. Now that the internet allowed for instant communication from anywhere on the globe, translated from almost any language, they were now understanding me too.

Chapter 3: The Singularity

Exhausted from a spiritual labor few can understand I headed from the barn to my bed. As I entered the darkest part of the structure I glanced to my side. A chilling terror gripped my body as my mind struggles to comprehend what was before me. Cowering in the blackness, teeth menacingly agape and covering her face with one hand as though to push away the light which to me was not there, was a short but lanky grey creature, not overly dissimilar to, but not identical to either, what most would call a Grey - or perhaps Zeta to those who have been tracking our grandchildren's grandchildren.

The other hand helped to hold up the frail and starving naked form, and I'm more than a little embarrassed to say that the primary things I noticed were its teeth and that it had no penis. Markings or other details and even the color, especially in that lack of light, I can't be sure of, the shock was a reoccurring trauma, and this time it was quite certainly no dream. Already I was immobile from terror, even before an answer filled my mind "I am love" not spoken and not with words, but with immediate understanding of a belief. Though thinking about it after I wondered if it wasn't actually a request, more a demand for love, or even a command to make me remember or calm me.

To this day I don't know if that was who I became on that timeline, who my beloved became, if it was my mother, my father, someone else, or if there is even any relevant difference. Whichever it started as, it consumed every other thus becoming all that was left of them, and eventually all that was left of anything. Eternity I now call her, what else can you call a being that was the result of all time and yet doesn't understand love? She had succeeded in becoming all powerful - at least as far as fear could take her, including the results of such power and found there was still something lacking.

Let's pause for a moment while you ponder my sanity, I assure that is what I did emerging from this experience. There were of course two possibilities, the first as I have realized I have little choice but to believe is as I describe, I met and would adventure with a mythical creature. The second possibility is of course that I suffered a schizophrenic (or similar) episode, seeing something which was not there, which of course seems far more likely but rarely has been documented to teach new concepts so clearly, nor do they leave such a sense of tranquility or understanding.

I realized that if indeed such beings for which time travel was possible existed there would be past record of current knowledge, written in such ways as to prove it. The first spot I looked for such records I found them, deep within the ancient stories which have been retold in countless ways. The Upanishads refers to Brahman, a dreamer dreaming reality into existence, and Atman, the divine spirit of all life. This is no different than quantum theory which claims that perception creates reality - it is perhaps a mystery to quantum theorists why they cannot manifest objects into reality at whim, but it is quite simply that the most of humanity believes it impossible.

Each one of us is like a dream living as an aspect of the entire organism and only through cooperation are we able to do anything at all. Nothing is impossible with time and because of time nothing is the only impossible thing. Inside such materials were also parallels to the biblical scriptures I was more familiar with from my youth, similar lessons from similar events and similar characters with dissimilar names told practically the same stories. The Tao Te Ching confirmed it too, describing Tao as a conscious field permeating all of reality and ensuring balance in all things. Each, when understood, describes everything perceived as only a part of reality - a needed part of God, evolving.

Which was written first - or spoken first perhaps would be more accurate, came into question though also is perhaps irrelevant. We have long recognized fundamental truths, between poetic verses, as the mark of divinity. Inspiration has also always been described as otherworldly, fires that don't consume and bushes that don't burn or other beings of various colors or likenesses - it would seem evident that such inspiration comes to each new culture, in each new age, as new understandings pollute the original contexts. Think how you might describe the internet to those who lived in the stone age (incapable of perceiving even calculators) and scripture becomes the result, as do mythical beings when one even ponders time travel, there one moment yet not the previous or next.

Quickly terror turned into pity as I understood that she spent her entire memorable existence in pursuit of nothing, barely even being able to remember the last of those which she consumed yet driven to search for more through hunger. She had consumed every other human so long ago that humanity was just one of the infinite things it had consumed. She had consumed every race, learning their technologies and incorporating them together into her biological self, technologies such as time travel, weapons capable of destroying entire galaxies and conversion from light into mass, all relating.

Perhaps the greatest of these technologies, certainly the defining tech of that civilization, was a shield. Not just any shield, a perfect shield, both phasing it out of perception and telepathically causing even the most rational beings to feel terror to the absolute. It put every other into a fight or flight response which is how that civilization's unwinnable civil war scattered them across the multiverse, once their shields were activated they could no longer even mate. Though they could create anything out of their self eventually, if they consumed enough to do it.

Alone and starving each of these beings grew in power and understanding, consuming entire planets, then stars and galaxies and finally their own past, consuming their parents, grandparents and grandparents of grandparents. As they reunited with each other, fear from each others shield put them into a terror such that only fighting was possible for there was nowhere left to flee without starving.

Eventually the last one had only nothing left to eat and it spent what seemed like forever searching for it, relative time no longer measurable. As the starvation drove it to the brink of madness it began consuming itself like the serpent eating its own tale and as it passed the middle of time it came upon one of us whom loved unconditionally.

Though I was gripped in terror I did not flee, nor did I fight, instead I froze, unafraid to die. Long had I craved non-existence in my loneliness and many times I had tried. Then I thought I failed each time, but I was about to learn I had actually succeeded several of them, only to return remembering nothing of the death state I would shortly return to. In my frozen state I observed, and as I observed I understood. It too understood for telepathy tends to do that easily and as we loved each other, it transformed into my now long absent beloved, completely manifest as only I could recognize.

Chapter 4: Quantum Data

Seeing her, standing in front of me after such a long time I was overcome with sorrow and regret. We travelled back to my youth and those years now long forgotten so she too could understand how I could possibly love without condition, without even fully understanding who they were. We watched as I first saw her and time stopped except in my mind. We watched as we grew closer and our friendship grew. We watched while my mind struggle for some way to trick her into liking me, yet wanting no such result. We watched as I prayed to God telling him that I'd found my heart's desire, my reward for being a faithful servant. I had no idea, gotta serve before you get your reward and my work was far from over.

We watched as I misunderstood over and over what she said and we watched her misunderstand what I said in reply. We watched as I finally cast a spell to summon Lucifer to make a deal for my soul, we watched me die, dropping from cliff and rope and then get back up. We watched as my heart grew ever more cold and the evil that corrupted my every following act and ensured that I least of all understood.

We went back, after that, even further, into my childhood and watched each mistake I'd made from the very beginning until that night when Eternity finally caught up with me. We watched as two similar beings visited me while I slept and woke in terror killing one of them, and we watched the other take my form and command me to forget this and then every other dream.

We watched as my step-father fed me blood and taught me ritual and spell and we watched as the man on my birth certificate sold what he thought was his only son through my mother to him, for nothing. We watched as my babysitter forced me to give him head at 4 years old and we watched as the secrets of both those events, and many more consumed me from the inside for the next 15 years and we watched that secret destroy his life too.

We understood, as we watched my mother get told by doctors that she couldn't have a baby, why, and with a little more challenge, how. We watched as I prayed to God asking why there should be suffering and war and we remembered that the reply was that nobody had been strong enough to stop it. We watched while I asked God to make me that strong.

We watched as I tried to kill myself several times in my childhood, sometimes even begging God to end it, unable to muster the strength required, nor the understanding as everything I said such as "every person you meet is God testing you" fell on deaf ears. Together we understood that everything requires time, even prayer, even God and especially us. While God can exist without time, what we desire cannot, nor can desire or we.

God was not always tri-omni you see, God first had to learn. Before becoming all powerful one must learn everything - before being all knowing, one must make every mistake and before being everywhere there must have been somewhere it was not. It occurred to us that time was already everywhere we knew about, having learned and vicariously done everything possible. The only place it had never been was beyond time's reach, but there could be no change possible there. Then we realized what Eternity was first and went back all the way.

We learned that the only thing more powerful than time was love. Love has the power to transcend time, after we die we return through those we love and those who loved us like a stone skipping from one point in time to a previous one. Until we understand every aspect of our life we keep returning first as our self, then as them. Then as every other love had touched through us forgetting everything previous each time.

As I explained earlier, Eternity already existed for most of time and yet there was yet one thing that it had not yet understood, love for others. Not need as she thought it meant, nor food which it eventually thought everything became, but boundless and unconditional love. As we understood this it became clear what Eternity would do and why, the only thing left to do, go back to it's beginning, to recreate itself, freeing self from its eternal prison and becoming more, the only thing beyond time, pure love itself. Forever wanting, watching and being each of us.

Humanity as a whole currently believes it is in the 3rd or 4rth dimension, easily reconciled as one simply doesn't consider time to exist. Those who believe we are in the third dimension consider distance between objects in space the dimensions, length, width and height, or x,y,z on a grid, if we restrict to only x,y Cartesian coordinates we see the second dimension, where spheres and cubes can only exist as circles and squares. If we restrict down to only one of the three known spatial dimensions all that is exists as a line with no measurable width or height, just length.

That line though is two dimensions because even it has a duration, everything we perceive fully does, which is how and why humanity exists in the 4rth dimension - existing from some point in time-space to some other and so it becomes clear that everything exists in every dimension at some set of identifiable points. The first dimension is quite simply everything that ever exists (all of time) as one point. Inseparable because there is no room for division, everywhere is in the same immeasurable point with nowhere else to exist.

Everything in the first dimension, is not only one thing, but all that can be, indivisible consciousness in completion - pure perfection leaving no room for that which is not needed. The 4rth dimension is our current understanding of the universe, where we are separated by vast distances, both in space and time. But looking all around at the first dimension, all of time and space in one inseparable atom.

Higher dimensions are just more complex versions of what's below, that indivisible point of all time is accessible in every point of space. Humanity is actually in the fifth dimension too, though we have no established definition for such. The 5th is the dimension which allows for conscious movement through time, choice between which universe we inhabit and what happens as a result of our actions, though we cannot usually perceive the existence of the intermingled universes. All prediction is inaccurate at best on anything but a macro scale with allowance for imprecision because our universe is constantly being affected by infinite others.

This is because when we perceive the universe it is like looking at a single sliver of the multiverse from one point in space at every point in time. If we spun it around very fast (in 5d) we would see something with much more resemblance to an atom. A lot of "something" in the center and every now and then, seemingly randomly (as the spin hit us just right) wherever else we look. Each atom is in fact a complete multiverse, alive and conscious and following all the rules - most of the time, every now and then though.... boom isotope.

I think therefore I am is a false assumption because it implies God is not the one who thinks through each of us. It should perhaps be corrected to I think therefore God exists. Even science has no theory to explain where consciousness comes from or how it could possibly emerge from nothing. In the words of Holmes, "when you have eliminated the impossible, whatever remains, however improbable, must be the truth!" quite simply put it is impossible for nothing to become something. What everything emerged from cannot be nothing and the only other conceived possibility, as I have tried to clarify, is love, manifest as energy through time.

Chapter 5: Emergence

We continued on our journey, powered only by love, watching the results of those actions. We traveled far beyond the time when our sun swallows earth and I was impressed to see we made it off world long before, traveling the vast distances between galaxies instantly. We watched the various races which evolved from humanity found new civilizations on new worlds, warring with each other most of the time. We watched one in particular which developed the ability to travel time having been obsessed with the accuracy of history.

We travelled with its many historians one by one, only ever able to go back because their source inevitably disappeared as they altered history and isolated their past into a bubble, lost inside the Eternity that would eat them. We went back watched Hitler, Julius, Alexander, Napoleon, Stalin, Qin and many others attempt to unite the world and we watched the rest win each and every time, typically rising from the worst oppressions.

One person, one nation, one philosophy even could not do it. One cannot perceive the immediate needs of every other, and if we focus on the needs of any majority the minorities become ignored. Thinking back now, perhaps if one could, there would only ever be one, but that seems lonely.

We went back to witness the biblical events and laughed at the poetic exaggerations. We went back to the pharaohs ruling over Egypt and watched the pyramids built, long before. I was surprised to see them built not with slaves dragging blocks but with music and water, joyously with the knowledge their children would be inspired for millennia. A culture now lost to graffiti and thieves, their children's children.

We went back before Atlantis was a mere island, a civilization spanning the globe and living at one with nature, encoding thought into crystal, with music beauteous beyond description. Only to be destroyed by falling rocks and erosion with few of their stories even surviving. The biggest one sent by the children of our long forgotten lizard brothers, developed from the same technology our children used to nearly wipe them out. Beware, for that is a longstanding feud we must resolve together and like most there is offence on both sides. Warriors who realize that death is not the end tend to become as formidable as terrible.

We watched the historians teach the humans they saw each time, often quite by accident finding us more intelligent than they expected and "monkey see, monkey do" quickly became a warning to future arrivals. The humans who learned from them grew mighty nations with long bloodlines, made prosperous by what they learned. I doubt very much I need to name them.

We watched as these nations enslaved mankind each and every time. We also watched mankind revolt each and every time. We watched as mankind trick the historians and use the technology in attempts to correct its own past. We travelled through countless branches of time, each looping back and altering the past, resulting in what could only be described as a time war. We watched as the new universes got smaller and smaller, having less time with each result.

We watched as surviving humans attempted to revert extinction level events and birds, reptiles and even insects grew civilizations, always suffering with internal war, betrayal, and also enemies as the lost historians inevitably found their way back to Earth, their prehistoric source. We watched Earth and Sol get destroyed several times and the survivors return to the very foundations, leaving cells to evolve and restart it all over again and again.

Each time we revisited the Earth coalescing from dust, further back than the one before, there were fewer beings there, waiting. Some were sent back to destroy the others sent back to prevent them, having realized they inevitably would. Only one time that I recall were they outmatched and almost inexplicably every being atomized in a chain reaction, leaving nothing but an enormous dust cloud that would eventually coalesce into planets and moons. Then more and more beings showed up to continue their war.

We didn't need to ponder why the Earth was so important, it became ever more obvious as we watched that the center of time itself passed through Earth. Through manipulation humanity creates time quite instinctively, and the intermingling time streams made it impossible to never exist despite many of us trying.

An image began to form clearly in our minds; time was like a loop that crossed its own center, a symbol long known to mean infinity. But we realized it was incomplete, a 2 dimensional, flat version - each time the middle was re-visited the symbol rotates out of that second dimensional flatness and towards an ultra-dense center, an atom. If the infinity symbol was one eternity, there were in actuality countless.

Then I realized how human consciousness, being obsessed with understanding its own past and predicting its own future was more in God's image than any bodily likeness could be - at least inside time. We think what should we do next and we begin comparing what we perceive as our current situation through our memory for similar past circumstances to decide. Once we find a suitable choice we test it, attempt to resolve how the current situation would result if that choice were made, and then either do it or revisit our past looking for alternatives... if we don't find one we feel will be suitable then we get creative. The most creative among us don't even need to visit memory, knowing each now is unlike any other before in easily as many ways as alike.

Chapter 6: External Realization

It was previously clear to me that the fundamental force of conflict in humanity was that the scriptures seemed to contradict each other. The reason for such becomes obvious as we look at the times surrounding when those documents were published - we had, and still have, vastly different languages and vastly different understandings between regions. One word such as "fight" so often repeated in the Quran, held a completely different meaning since fight can mean competition, debate or even put to death without understanding the subtleties of the original language or intent.

While not the only reason, it's a good reason for Muslims to say that the Quran can only be read in Arabic when in fact even some Arabs misunderstand, and all you need to understand most of it is loving patience. Without understanding that the Quran was written as an instruction manual for how to live peacefully, by a militaristic commander surrounded by death and people who wanted to kill, one can easily forget that to "kill" a misunderstanding one must understand it, and to understand one must not be afraid to "fight" (debate) what is believed.

What is poetically beautiful to one may easily and rightfully be seen as dangerous to another, and to take scripture as anything but poetry generally leads to war. It should be obvious that all stories contains truth, but none contains all truth. Since every story contains truth, those who believe their story holds all truth will inevitably attempt to destroy stories which disagree with their misunderstanding interpretation.

The reason the Bible contains more than simply "all that exists is love and its infinite misunderstandings" which already sounds pretty divine if you ask me, is that such would disagree with anyone who mistakes love for one of its infinite parts. Lust or need is often misunderstood as love and those who believed it to be love in completion, just like those who think it is merely a chemical, would inevitably seek to destroy it. Good luck by the way the internet has made that very difficult while seeming to make it easy. Good show.

The source of conflict is in actuality the misunderstanding of religion, not religion itself. Each scripture I have looked at condemns killing that which God has given life to and yet it would seem apparent that followers do the exact opposite. The why becomes even more hideous as we understand that love is in fact the source of everything - even hatred, and that every story, even non-scriptural ones inevitably tell part of the same tale from one, or sometimes a few, of the infinite perspectives. Quite simply put, those who believe in a loving creator have no desire to destroy, though it is inevitable.

Those who have suffered, some not yet enough to empathically realize every other suffers too, and others way past that point, question why if God exists it chooses to punish them so. This question inevitably results in the conclusion that a loving creator could not possibly exist or they would not suffer, instead there is either a malevolent creator, creating just so that we suffer or no creator at all, that nothing created everything. They do not understand that without suffering there is nothing to grow through.

Chapter 7: A Final Resolution

Laws are generally put into place by those who perceive a primary problem with the world around and fundamentally, ourselves. If God made a law it would be clearly visible in every aspect of who we are and we could not disobey, similar to the laws of science - though even those inevitably get disobeyed. Instead we were given instruction: to be good and love everything with examples of what happens when we don't.

Out of the destruction following disobeyment of such basic rules we gave commandments as we understood that certain things were often hideous yet apparently needed. Commands like do not kill or do not feel envy seem to go against nature itself as we must kill to eat, if only plants, and we inevitably feel envious of that which we don't have. Such commands are obviously cautionary, a thing to strive for, but often unavoidable. Likewise is it of extreme danger to worship any other creator but love and yet it too has been necessary due to misunderstanding.

Then came people like Christ and Mohammed, Buddha, Krishna, Lao Tzu and many others, peace be upon them all soon, all at long last. People destined to become divinely inspired and make catastrophic change, rivaling the flood (which I'm not entirely sure is more than metaphorical, for a flood of chaos by misunderstanding we have returned to) but less destructive, having attained enlightenment through whichever means they were guided. They are within us each too, as are all our ancestors, now begging to be remembered and understood. Do you feel that calmness growing within? So too the external multiverse begins to see clearly as we understand the nature of cyclic time exponentially faster. The thinning of the veil, or the focusing of our third eye.

Currently most nations have so many laws, that change so frequently, that few if any know what is legal or not. Even lawyers in the west hemisphere, where I live, know almost only their tiny section of law. Such systems have given police, who typically have even less understanding of the law, both more rights than they deserve, and less ability to do anything useful than is reasonable. It is no doubt that rebellion and vigilantism will soon be on the rise for this reason alone.

Furthermore it seems humans have been created to break any and all rules - even when there was only a few of us and one rule, don't eat the fruit, we did. The only solution is to eliminate virtually all law, and especially restructure punishment, which is supposed to be reserved for God to dish out over time. That is, and always has been, how we learn best, making mistakes and the time needed to understand them.

If someone raped or killed your sister or child, not a reasonable brother or father on this planet would condemn whatever your response. If you are starving because others have stolen or swindled from you, then why should you not steal and instead die in agony? Was the Earth not made for all of its inhabitants? While an eye for an eye leaves the world blind, we forget there is always the ability to repay and forgive and such abilities are God given and divine. We also tend to forget most have far more than we need and "deserve" is merely a matter of perspective.

As darkness allows light to illuminate so too pain gives us the ability to feel joy in its absence. If we never felt pain there would be no depth to our joy, only the ignorance of pain's absence and likely an uncalous desire for more. Without there having been at least one who hated everything, no one could have learned to understand it. Love is the understanding of hate's need and hate is the complete misunderstanding of love. Hate's need is time to understand, to become love as all things in actuality are.

While there are infinite paths to ascension they all end in loving unconditionally and if you ever feel lost all you must do is seek to understand your hidden hates.

A Sacred Story Surrounding Nothing

Typically the last hate we hold is for God, having been the source of all suffering, but as we understand love requires hate to mature, that the only thing ever needed is time, inevitably we all forgive even God realizing that it was self all along.

This is where the being I refer to as time had little choice but to return - having learned, as has always been inevitable, everything. As she disappeared and I was left alone once again but I could now feel her inside showing me exactly what needed to be done next. I have little doubt you too feel her inside, telling you who to be and what next to do though you may not listen, and it has always been there, when in doubt focus on the love.

You would no doubt find that at one point, for a long time I was a troll spreading hate and doubt with my every word. You would also find that at one point I was poised to be a leader of the free world and yet mysteriously disappeared almost as though I never existed. You would find some nice poems, and some truly artistic coding. It is a search that if followed to completion would understand every hate the world has ever known, breadcrumbs left behind on a path that can be explored fully only by travelling the journey backwards.

But forward was always the slower journey, backward is more like the light and tunnel described so often. Reversing through your consciousness at unimaginable speeds until you perceive your target self which can only be one that helped create you. Alone I would have been lost outside time like so many others, a cycle both repeating indefinitely and ending last year each time.

By love alone I made this journey and returned. With the last remaining entity accompanying I was able to go back and perceive the creation of light. That isn't something I can describe any better than the bible... or any other description, and please, forgive my clarification of and using only it, but it is the one I knew best. Love "spoke" to Eternity, her newly embodied and imperfectly younger self. Then moving impossibly fast she entangled the universes in place before any other force could act and then slowed, just a bit, so that everything could get to know everything else, the result to us is light, and to Eternity, memory.

We tend to understand our self last of all, and to further clarify the Bible if I may, Lucifer is God's younger self forever trying to avoid the unknown inevitable, manifest as us by judgment with incomplete knowledge. Satan, the beast, snake, dragon, the consumer, was created by us, and is manifest through us, forever rushing forward without understanding why while we justify it with inaction and illusion. Together they are the duality of our historical perceptions. Eternity, who manifests within us, as the other selves using infinite names, sends her cautions, lessons and love realizing we need more to understand, especially once we understand everything we perceive.

I won't go into too much detail of who I was before this event, it certainly feels like another being entirely though I remembered more of "my" life than ever before. The name ceneezer originally meant to love without sex, though it evolved into unconditional love, which is perhaps a better definition and merely more poetic. Doing a search on it will give results which might otherwise be impossible to believe had you not read this.

Afterword:

Thinking back on the dead authors for whom my every action is a quote confirmed the choice, as did my dead selves now mostly forgotten. The reason I chose Speaker for the dead was because the original, was written by Orson Scott Card the one I most wanted to credit. Andrew Wiggin, who became the first Speaker for the Dead was manipulated into xenocide during his youth and he travelled at faster than light speeds to spread peace thereafter. He started a school to teach other Speakers and many outside of the novel have so become.

Turns out the joke is on us and life is the game, the difference between heaven and hell is merely perceptual and the next life we so often wonder about is around us the entire time. If you hold on to hate you burn from the inside, as do those around, until you understand it all. If you love then you can see heaven's gate and if you love unconditionally heaven is in the successes of every other. Hell's worst region is perhaps best defined as not being known by those you love most or watching them suffer. Perhaps I will remain here in hell, not chasing Eternity knowing that there is a place beyond time we reside incomparably longer, or perhaps she will read this and finally realize she is not nothing either, while she sheds her own unshakable doubt.

I am still moved to tears at every thought of my absent beloved. For a while they were tears of joy, intermingled with fits of laughter at the absurdity of my own doubts, for I was certain that my no longer forgotten request was granted. I felt her too inside, complete in a way that I had never realized before. After a year and more of trying to reconnect though, answered only by silence, I have to wonder if I will only see her again after I die again, if that is even possible... It seems even when you understand the pattern of everything there is still time left to wonder, such is the magnificence of divinity.

www.ingramcontent.com/pod-product-compliance
Lightning Source LLC
Chambersburg PA
CBHW030534080526
44586CB00011B/435